Going for a Walk

Deborah Chancellor
Photography by Chris Fairclough

W
FRANKLIN WATTS
LONDON • SYDNEY

This edition 2005

Franklin Watts
338 Euston Road
London NW1 3BH

Franklin Watts Australia
Level 17/207 Kent Street
Sydney, NSW 2000

ISBN: 978 0 7496 6112 0
Dewey Decimal Classification 912
A CIP record for this book is available from the British Library

Printed in Malaysia

Series editor: Sarah Peutrill
Series design: Peter Scoulding
Design: Hardlines
Photographs: Chris Fairclough
Consultant: Steve Watts

Bus map supplied courtesy of Centro
Street map reproduced by permission of Geographers' A-Z Map Co. Ltd. Licence No.
B1287. This product includes mapping data licensed from Ordnance Survey®. © Crown
Copyright 2001. Licence number 100017302

With grateful thanks to Gillian, Harry and Edward.

Franklin Watts is a division of Hachette Children's Books.

Contents

Going Out

It is ten o'clock on Saturday morning. Harry and Edward are going out for a walk with their mum.

The family live in a street called York Road. This street is in King's Heath, in the south of a big **city** called Birmingham.

If you look at a map of Great Britain, Birmingham is in the centre of England. It is in a **region** called the Midlands.

Country maps of Britain have to fit a lot of land into a small space. Maps like this are on a very small **scale**.

York Road

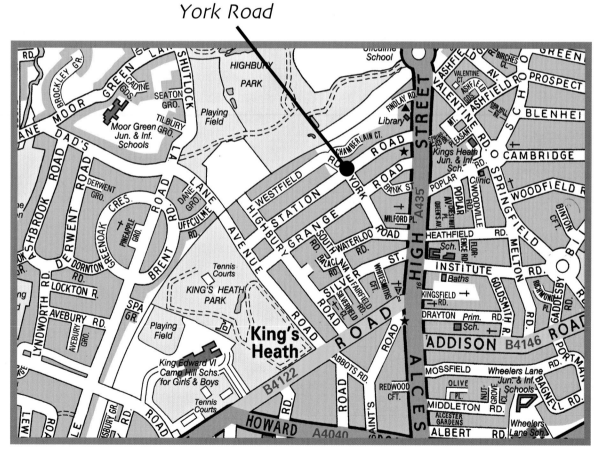

Street maps, like this, give much more detail than country maps. They show every road in an area and are on a large scale.

Down the Road

Harry, Edward and Mum turn left out of their gate and walk along York Road. They pass some houses and then some shops.

They cross the road to look in the window of a pet shop. For the children, this is an important **feature** of their **local area**.

The pet shop is a three-minute walk from where the family live.

The family cross back over York Road and continue towards the High Street.

You can follow each stage of the family's **route** on very large-scale maps like this one.

They cross the road to look at the pet shop.

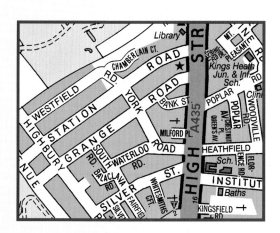

The pet shop is not labelled on the street map of King's Heath. On this map, only street names, schools and **public buildings** are shown.

On the High Street

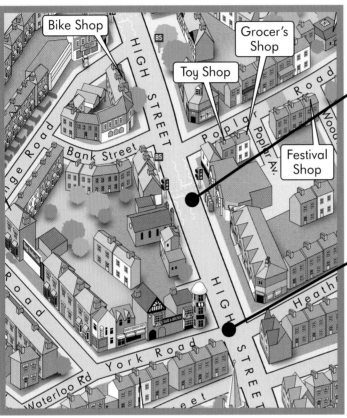

The pedestrian crossing is here.

The family turn left here into the High Street.

At the end of York Road they turn left into the High Street. There is a lot of traffic, because this is a **major road** that leads into Birmingham city centre.

They cross the High Street safely at a **pedestrian crossing**.

Harry and Edward count lots of buses passing by. Several bus routes pass through the High Street in King's Heath.

Look at this **bus route** map. It is a very simple map showing only the roads that are on a bus route.

Each bus has its own number. The numbers on the map tell you which buses go along each road.

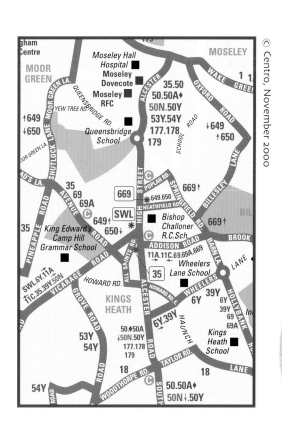

Along Poplar Road

POPLAR RD 14

The family keep walking along the High Street. They turn right into Poplar Road. It is quieter than the High Street, although there are still some interesting shops to look at along the way.

Harry and Edward would like to go into this toy shop on Poplar Road.

The family turn right here.

They visit the grocer's shop, which is next to the toy shop.

12

Mum needs to go to a **grocer's shop** called 'Caribbean Sam' to buy some food. The family walk a short distance up Poplar Road to reach the shop. They stop there for a while to chat with the shopkeeper.

CARIBBEAN
SAM
Specialising in
HARD DOUGH
BREAD
BULLA CAKES
BUNS
etc

This grocer's shop sells food from the Caribbean. Big cities like Birmingham offer a wide choice of food from all over the world.

Looking at Landmarks

Harry, Edward and Mum come out of the grocer's shop. As they walk up Poplar Road, they can see a church in the distance. It is a big church with a tall spire.

*King's Heath Methodist Church is a local **landmark**. It is easy to find on a street map.*

The church is next to a **roundabout** and opposite a school. Maps use **symbols** to show certain things, such as churches. These are explained in a **key** to the map, for example † = church. Can you find this church on the map?

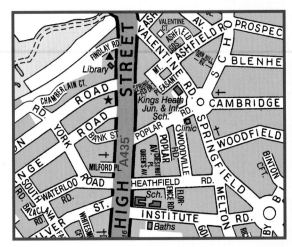

14

The family cross Poplar Avenue and continue along Poplar Road. Opposite the church they can now see a roundabout and a school.

This is the view from the church.

The school is here.

The church is here.

Back up Poplar Road

Towards the end of Poplar Road the family visit the festival shop. This shop sells things to celebrate different festivals, from countries around the world.

The festival shop sells many interesting and unusual things.

The festival shop is just before Woodville Road.

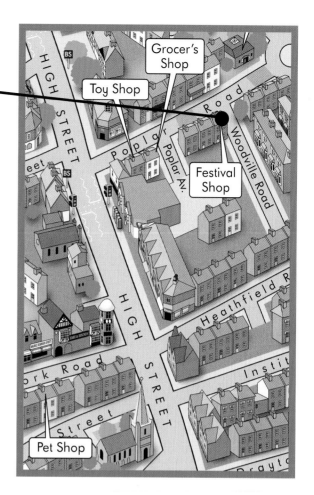

After leaving the shop, the children decide it is time to go to the park. They turn back and walk in the opposite **direction** up Poplar Road. Walking this way, they can see the High Street ahead of them.

The family can see the High Street again at the end of Poplar Road.

Towards Grange Road

Distance walked: 700 m. **Time:** 10.31 am

The family turn left into the High Street. They cross the road again at the pedestrian crossing. At this point they turn right to go back up the High Street, away from York Road. They cross over Bank Street.

The bike shop on the High Street is close to the turning into Grange Road.

The word 'Road' has been shortened to 'RD' on this sign.

Harry and Edward see a street sign for 'Grange Road' on a wall, at the **junction** of the High Street and Grange Road. This is the road they need to take to get to the park.

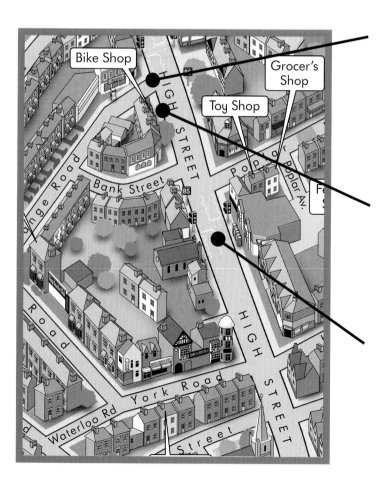

This is where Grange Road meets the High Street.

The family stop to look at some bikes here.

The pedestrian crossing is here.

Close to Home

Mum, Harry and Edward turn left into Grange Road. They cross Bank Street again.

There are no shops on Grange Road, and the family walk past a row of houses with small front gardens. Cars are parked beside the pavement.

They turn left here.

This is where the family cross York Road.

Soon they reach a **crossroads**. The road they cross is their own street, York Road. As they cross the road, the family home is on their left. It is not far away.

The family must continue straight on down Grange Road to get to the park.

A Long Road

Distance walked: 1.35 km. Time: 10.48 am

It takes the family about ten minutes to walk the rest of Grange Road. On a street map of King's Heath, Grange Road looks short, but Harry and Edward think it is a very long road!

AVENUE RD 14

At the end of Grange Road, the family cross over Avenue Road to reach the park.

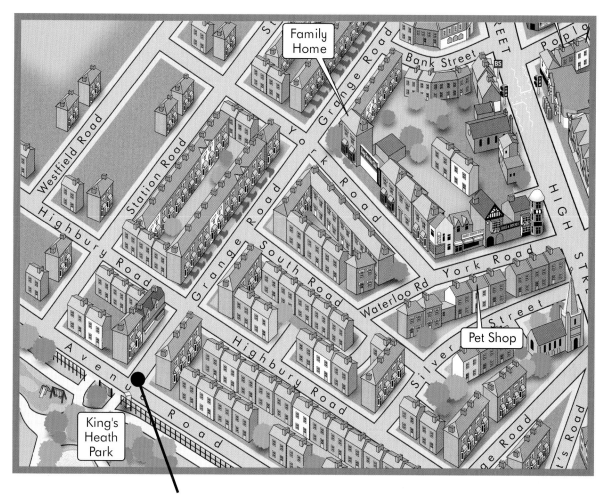

The family cross here to get to the park.

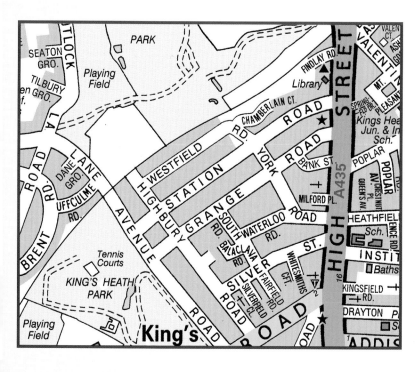

This street map also shows Grange Road. On this map Grange Road looks shorter. The map has less detail and is on a smaller scale than the map at the top of the page.

At the Park

Distance walked: 1.55 km. Time: 11.00 am

When the family arrive at King's Heath Park, they walk to the playground.

The park gates are here.

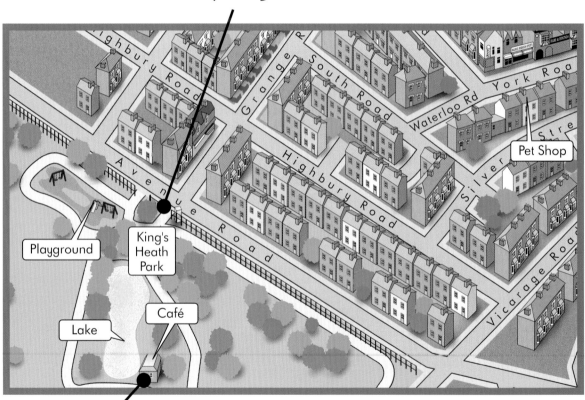

The family go to this café.

Parks are often found in the centre of busy cities. On maps, they can be seen as wide open, green spaces in the middle of built-up areas. City parks give people a chance to relax, away from noisy streets and traffic.

First the children play on the swings. Then they all walk to the park café. They stop to look at the lake on the way. In the café mum treats Harry and Edward to a drink and a snack.

In the park, the children notice that the autumn leaves are changing colour.

The family have enjoyed their time in the park, but it is time for them to go home. Look at the map on the next page. Can you work out the route they took?

Follow the Map

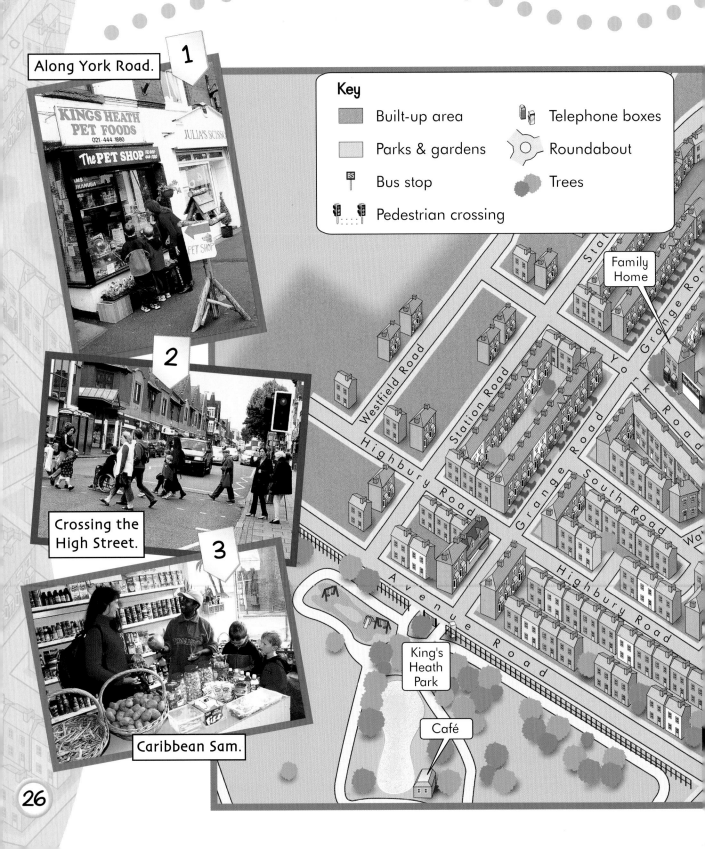

1 Along York Road.

2 Crossing the High Street.

3 Caribbean Sam.

Key

- Built-up area
- Parks & gardens
- BS Bus stop
- Pedestrian crossing
- Telephone boxes
- Roundabout
- Trees

Family Home

Westfield Road

Station Road

Highbury Road

Grange Road

York Road

Grange Road

South Road

Highbury Road

Avenue Road

King's Heath Park

Café

KINGS HEATH PET FOODS
021·444 1880
The PET SHOP

JULIA'S SCISSORS

Look again at the family's route. They saw many things on their walk. They went along busy roads and quiet streets, passing a variety of houses and shops. Can you find on the map where each of these photos was taken? What do you see on the way to your local park?

4 Back on the High Street.

5 Along Grange Road.

6 In the park.

School

Church

Grocer's Shop

Toy Shop

e Shop

Festival Shop

Pet Shop

Poplar Road

Poplar Av.

Woodville Road

Springfield Road

Melton Road

Heathfield Road

Institute Road

Drayton Road

Addison Road

Mossfield Road

HIGH STREET

All Saint's Road

Activities

Work it out

1. Look at page 10. Why is there so much traffic on the High Street? Where is the safest place to cross the roa

2. Look at page 16. Would you see a festival shop like thi in a village? What kind of shops might be in a village? How are they different from the shops you find in a ci

3. Look at the two maps on page 23. Find Grange Road o each map. Why does it look shorter on one map?

Make a Land Use Map

- Think about your route to school.
- Write a list of all the different types of building you pass on the way, such as houses, shops and offices.
- Draw a map of your route to school. Draw boxes on the map for each of the buildings on your list.
- Use a different colour for each type of building.
- Make a key to explain your map.

Glossary

bus route
The way a bus goes to get from one place to another, stopping at particular points along the way. A bus will always follow the same route.

city
A big, important town where lots of people live.

crossroads
The point where different roads cross each other.

direction
The way in which you are moving or pointing.

feature
An interesting or important part of something.

grocer's shop
A shop that sells food, drink and other useful things for your house.

junction
The point where different roads meet.

key
A guide to explain the symbols on a map.

landmark
Something that is easy to recognise.

local area
The land around a particular place.

major road
A very busy road, often the main route from one place to another.

pedestrian crossing
A place where people can cross the road safely.

public building
A building that is open to everyone, such as a library or post office.

region
A part of a country.

roundabout
A road junction where the traffic has to go round in a circle.

route
A way from one place to another.

scale
The size used to show an area of land on a map, compared to the size of that land in real life. Small-scale maps show more land than large-scale maps.

street map
A map that shows all the roads in a town or city.

symbol
A simple picture on a map that stands for something, such as † = a church.

Index

About this Book

FOLLOW THE MAP is designed as a first introduction to map skills. The series is made up of familiar journeys that the young reader is encouraged to follow. In doing so the child will begin to develop an understanding of the relation between maps and the geographical environment they describe. Here are some suggestions to gain the maximum benefit from GOING FOR A WALK.

Throughout the book, the reader is introduced to some basic geographical concepts and associated vocabulary (for example the concept of land use in cities). This will provide a useful foundation for more complex exploration of these ideas at a later stage.

A number of different types of map are illustrated in the book. It is helpful to expose the young reader to a wide variety of geographical resources. Build up a collection of maps of the child's local area, and discuss their different purposes.

On pages 7 and 23, the child is invited to compare maps of different scales. The concept of scale is a difficult one for the child to grasp, and these pages should provide a basis for further discussion. It may be useful to look at different scale maps of the child's local environment.

On page 14, map symbols are brought to the child's attention. Explore this subject further by discussing a range of symbols shown on different maps.

Encourage the child to describe his or her own journey to a local park, using the appropriate geographical vocabulary. Discuss the similarities and/or differences with the walk illustrated in the book.